STRANGE STORIES
But True

KING TUT'S CURSE

AMAZING ATHLETIC FEATS

MONSTER OR MYTH?

. . . AND MORE

BY
Janice Greene

SADDLEBACK
EDUCATIONAL PUBLISHING

STRANGE But True STORIES

BOOK 1

The Presidential Ghost
Mystery Spots on Earth
UFO or Weather Balloon?

BOOK 3

The Jersey Devil
Phantom Ships
Living Dinosaurs?

BOOK 2

Bob Lazar, the UFO Guy
The Mothman Mystery
Mischievous Spirits

BOOK 4

What Lurks Beneath the Waves?
Winchester Mystery House
Skulls of Doom

BOOK 5

King Tut's Curse
Amazing Athletic Feats
Monster or Myth?

AND MUCH MORE!

Development and Production: Laurel Associates, Inc.
Cover Design: IQ Design, Inc.
Cover Photograph: Brian Philip Davis, www.brianphilipdavis.com

SADDLEBACK
EDUCATIONAL PUBLISHING
Three Watson
Irvine, CA 92618-2767
Website: www.sdlback.com

ISBN-13: 978-1-59905-014-0
ISBN-10: 1-59905-014-5
eBook: 978-1-60291-434-6

Printed in the United States of America

13 12 11 10 09   3 4 5 6 7 8 9

CONTENTS

GREAT IMPOSTERS

THE MAN OF MANY FACES

Ferdinand Waldo Demara had lied and cheated all his life. But he'd also helped many people. So what do you think? Was he a good man—or a sick liar?

Demara was born in Massachusetts, in 1921. His family was wealthy, and life was comfortable. At school, Demara wasn't a great student, but he read books on a great many subjects. And he also had a photographic memory, which made learning much easier.

In 1932, the Depression wiped out his father's business. Suddenly, the family was poor. Demara lost the comfortable life he knew, as well as his social status. These losses affected him deeply.

As a teenager, he left home and joined a monastery. But a monk's life was too quiet for him, and he didn't stay long.

5

When the Japanese bombed Pearl Harbor on Dec. 7, 1941, Demara was eager to serve his country. He joined the navy, but soon became bored with navy life. One day, he had a meeting with the base commander. When the commander wasn't looking, Demara lit a match soaked with paraffin. He dropped the match into a wastebasket and watched the papers burst into flames. During the confusion that followed, Demara made his move. He stole official stationery from the commander's desk and quickly tucked it in his shirt.

Soon after that, Demara faked his own death. Everyone thought he'd drowned. Then he wrote letters on the official navy stationery to create a new identity—Dr. Robert Linton French.

As Dr. French, Demara got a job at a college in Pennsylvania. Although he'd barely finished high school, he was now head of the school of psychology. Then, unfortunately for Demara, the navy tracked him down. He spent the next 18 months in a military prison.

In 1950, Demara was hired as an administrator at the Notre Dame Normal School in Maine. Why not? He had papers to prove that he was a zoologist and a cancer researcher. His new name was Dr. Cecil Hamann.

Demara became friends with Dr. Joseph Cyr, a Canadian doctor. Demara promised to help him get a license to practice medicine in the United States. Give your credentials to me, Demara said, and I'll make sure they get into the right hands. But Dr. Cyr had no idea who he was dealing with. Demara took the papers and used them to join the Royal Canadian Navy—as a doctor.

Soon Demara was on board a navy ship. The Korean War was raging as the ship headed in that direction. Now Demara faced the biggest challenge of his life. He had to treat people's illnesses and injuries—without having one minute of training or practice! One day the ship's captain complained about his three impacted teeth. Moments before taking them out, Demara grabbed a medical book and read what to do.

One night, during a violent storm, 16 South Korean soldiers came on board. All were wounded; all needed attention. Demara picked shrapnel from their wounds, then cleaned and bandaged them. He stopped arteries from bleeding. He successfully collapsed the lung of a soldier who had tuberculosis. Then he opened up a soldier's chest and removed a bullet lodged close to his heart. By then, he'd read quite a lot about medical care.

Demara admitted later that he'd prayed he wouldn't kill anyone. Yet all the while he felt a self-confidence he couldn't understand. And he found the experience tremendously exciting.

He continued working as a doctor in Korea. People loved him. But meanwhile, back in Canada, the real Doctor Cyr kept hearing about the wonderful work he was doing in Korea, so he called the Royal Canadian Navy. Demara insisted he was really Dr. Hamann. But the navy soon realized his story was false, and Demara was dismissed.

In 1952, Demara sold his story to a popular magazine for $2,500. He sent all but $500 to his mother.

The magazine story caused Demara problems. Now, when he'd create a new identity and apply for a job, many people already knew who he was.

Demara then applied for a job in the Texas prison system. As references he listed Dr. Hamann and a child counselor named Fred Demara. Using the name Ben W. Jones, he got the job. He rose quickly in the ranks of the prison system. Finally, he became an assistant warden. But then a prisoner recognized him from the magazine story. Demara sneaked away in the night before he was caught.

Later, Demara was arrested for

forgery, theft, and being drunk in public. But the state of Texas dropped all charges against him. Why? People there were quite embarrassed that Demara had managed to fool prison officials.

Calling himself Frank Kingston, Demara next found work at a school for the mentally retarded in New York. One day he heard about a school in the little island town of North Haven, Maine. The school desperately needed a teacher. If it didn't get one fast it would be forced to close.

In the summer of 1956, Demara arrived at North Haven. He was now posing as Martin Godgart, a highly qualified teacher.

The islanders loved him. They felt he was a truly gifted teacher.

Outside of class, Demara helped children with their reading lessons. He urged his students to read everything they could get their hands on. He organized kids to fix up the homes of elderly widows, and he ran a bible school. He also started a Sea Scout unit for teenage boys.

One of his students, David Cooper, remembered Demara's photographic memory. Cooper said, "When the mail arrived by boat, we'd have Mr. Godgart skim a magazine. Later we'd test him on it. He'd repeat the articles word for word!"

It wasn't long, though, before Demara became restless. He started to behave strangely, even at school. One of his students, Eric Hopkins, recalled that time. "One day he pulled a loaded gun, a little black revolver, out of his pocket. He put it on the table for us boys to see. Just then my mother walked in. She was shocked when she saw the gun."

Hopkins' mother, June, had already been wondering about Godgart. He'd often been a dinner guest at their home. After several beers, his stories about his past seemed to change. A couple of times, he'd showed them the picture of himself from the magazine article. (He had cut off

the captions.) He'd tease the family, saying, "Wouldn't you like to know?"

June Hopkins sent away for a copy of the magazine. When she discovered who Martin Godgart really was, she found a way to get Demara's fingerprints. The next time he came to the house, June Hopkins saved his water glass. Then she sent it to investigators at the state capital. They compared the prints from the glass to the prints in Demara's criminal record. Of course, the prints matched.

On Feb. 14, 1957, two state police detectives arrived at the school. As they approached him, Demara asked, "What took you so long to get here?"

The detectives took Demara away. He walked out silently—not saying so much as a goodbye to anyone.

In court, Demara pleaded guilty to being a fake. But, he argued, he hadn't done anything to hurt anyone.

The judge took pity on him. "This has to stop somewhere," he said, "even if your motives were good." He placed Demara on probation.

After Demara left the island, he was in the spotlight again. Newspapers told the story of the Great Imposter. Twice more he was featured in national magazines. He also appeared on TV. In 1959, his biography was published. And in 1961, a movie of his life story called *The Great Imposter* hit the theaters. Demara was actually famous for being himself!

But when the thrill of fame wore off, Demara became deeply unhappy. He called the Hopkins family and told them they were being watched. He tried a few more disguises. In 1970, he became the Reverend Fred Demara, the minister of a church in Washington.

Then he dropped out of sight until 1982, when he died in California. His doctor remembered him as "the most miserable, unhappy man I ever knew."

Eric Hopkins, his former student, said, "To tell the truth, I was happy when

I heard he'd died. A lot of people really liked him—but in no way was he the folk hero some people made him out to be. He actually scared us as kids. I lived with a subconscious fear of him for a long time after he left."

Another resident of North Haven, Lewis Haskell, had a different opinion. "Whoever he was, he was the best," Haskell said. "I'm honored to have known him, and to have been deceived by him."

A FAMOUS DOCTOR'S SECRET

In 1816, Dr. James Barry arrived at the Cape of Good Hope on the southern tip of Africa. He said he'd trained as a doctor at Edinburgh University, in Scotland. He had three years of medical experience in the army. He also said that he was only 17 years old. No one knew who his parents were, or where he had grown up.

Dr. Barry made powerful friends. One of them was Lord Charles Somerset, the British governor of the Cape. Soon after

Dr. Barry arrived, Lord Somerset made him his personal physician.

Dr. Barry proved his skill quickly. When one of Lord Somerset's daughters seemed certain to die, Dr. Barry saved her life. That made him a favorite of the wealthy and powerful families of the Cape.

Dr. Barry was also a favorite with women, but he never married. Some described him as being "every inch a gentleman." Many found him kind and caring. But others thought he was vain and disagreeable.

At the age of 23, Dr. Barry was appointed colonial medical inspector. That job gave him a great deal of power. He made more friends—and enemies.

For one thing, he angered army doctors by speaking out against the filthy conditions in military hospitals.

Dr. Barry complained about poor conditions in leper colonies and insane asylums. He also worked to improve the lives of poor, black Africans. The wealthy

white people of the Cape resented this.

Some of his ideas about health were very modern. He realized that crowded living conditions, poor diet, and poor sanitation made people sick. At the time, most people simply didn't think this way.

Finally, Dr. Barry's enemies got him removed from his job. So he left the Cape to work in other countries.

When the Crimean War broke out in 1853, he was living in Greece. He was refused permission to work at the front. So he asked that wounded soldiers be sent to his hospital in Greece.

After several months, soldiers began arriving at Dr. Barry's hospital. War wounds were only part of their suffering. Starvation, cholera, dysentery, fever, and frostbite were common conditions. But Dr. Barry was somehow able to save most of them. Of the 462 men who came to his hospital, only 17 died.

When it came time for Dr. Barry to go on vacation, he went to Crimea instead.

There he met the famous nurse, Florence Nightingale.

Barry and Nightingale shared many of the same beliefs. They both thought that good food, good hygiene, and fresh air helped people stay healthy. Both did all they could to help the ordinary soldier. And both were impatient with medical officials' stubborn reluctance to change. As Florence Nightingale put it, they were mostly interested in keeping themselves "out of the blame."

In 1859, Barry returned to Britain. At age 60, he retired, and six years later, he died. His death was written up in Charles Dickens' magazine *All Year Around*.

Dr. Barry had said that when he died, he wanted to be buried in the clothes he had on. The death certificate was issued. A woman laid out the body—and only then was the doctor's secret discovered.

Doctor Barry was a woman.

How could anyone have guessed that Dr. Barry was a female? Certainly, he was a small, delicate-looking man. But in those days, there were no woman doctors. In fact, it was believed that women weren't even capable of being doctors! So no one thought to question Dr. Barry. She was able to live a lie for many, many years.

THE LOST PRINCESS

In 1918, the Russian revolution was raging. The Bolsheviks had captured the Russian royal family. They were being held prisoner at a house in the town of Yekaterinburg. Then, on July 16, the Bolsheviks shot them all: Nicholas II, Alexandra, and their children. Yet the bodies weren't found until 60 years later! For more than ten years, the two men who discovered the bodies were afraid to talk. Without evidence, no one could prove that the entire family was dead. Rumors flew.

Most of the rumors were centered on the youngest child—a 17-year-old girl named Anastasia.

In 1921, a young woman in a German mental hospital refused to say her name. Then one day, the nameless patient saw an article titled, "Did Anastasia Survive the Massacre?" Along with the article was a picture of the princess. A nurse, Anna Chemnitz, remembered the patient asking, "Can't you see the similarity between us two?"

Soon several Russian exiles came to the mental hospital to meet her. These people had fled their homes and their country when the Bolsheviks took over. Now they arrived, one after another, hoping to see their lost princess, Anastasia. For these Russian exiles, Anastasia was a link to the past, to the lives they once led. To the rest of the world, Anastasia was a romantic figure. She was the royal princess who had somehow escaped death and then re-appeared! It seemed like a miracle.

The young woman's story was this: She had not been killed, but wounded.

Along with her mother and sisters, she had hidden jewels in her corset. When the Bolsheviks fired at them, she said, the bullets bounced off their clothes.

According to the young woman, a palace guard found that she was still alive. He smuggled her into Romania, where she later married him.

After he was killed in a street fight with Bolsheviks, she traveled to Berlin. Her goal was to find her grandmother, the Empress. But the Empress refused to see her. The girl was so downhearted, she tried to kill herself. That's how she ended up in a mental hospital—and eventually forgot who she was.

Russian exiles spent hours with the young woman, who now called herself Anna Anderson. They reminisced about Russia's royal court in the "old days." Through Anna Anderson, the exiles remembered their world, which was gone forever. After finding her a home, they helped Anna Anderson try to prove that she was truly Anastasia.

Anna's fame grew as her portrait appeared on chocolate boxes and cigarette packs. There were three movies about her, a play, and many books.

One day a Baroness Buxhoeveden came to see her. The Baroness had been a lady-in-waiting to a powerful family of the old royal court. She claimed that Anderson was a fraud. In turn, Anna said she was afraid of the baroness, because she'd betrayed the royal family.

Then, in 1927, a story appeared in a German newspaper. A young Berlin woman had recognized Anna Anderson as her former roommate. She said that Anna Anderson was really Franziska Schanzkowska, a Polish factory worker.

But Anna Anderson stood firm. She insisted she was really Anastasia. And who could prove her wrong? The bodies of the royal family had not been found. And the Russian government was silent on the subject.

For years, to keep people aware of her story, Anderson tried to prove she was Anastasia. By 1968, perhaps she was tired of her efforts. She went to live in the United States. There she met and married a rich historian, Jack Manahan. Her husband believed her story. They lived in Charlottesville, Virginia, until her death in 1984.

In 1991, the bones of the royal family were found at last. By this time, scientists were able to use DNA samples. There was no doubt that this was the royal family.

While living in the United States, Anna had surgery. A bit of tissue from that operation had been saved at the hospital.

Scientists compared Anderson's DNA to that of the royal family. There was no match. Instead, the DNA actually proved that Anna Anderson was Franziska Schanzkowska.

The tests persuaded *almost* everyone. But Anderson had convinced hundreds of people that she was, indeed, the princess Anastasia. Many relatives of the royal family and the family's household staff believed her. These were people who would have known Anastasia as a child. It even seems likely that Franziska Schanzkowska herself believed that she was Anastasia.

SPORTS SHORTS

THE BATTLE OVER BOXING

The boxing match between Jim Corbett and Charley Mitchell was more than a fight between two men. It was a battle between local citizens and the governor of Florida. It also pitted a sheriff against an athletic club.

The match almost sparked a battle between Florida and Georgia!

Most of the conflict took place before the match even got started.

The story began in September 1892, when James J. Corbett won the U.S. heavyweight championship. Corbett beat John L. Sullivan in a 21-round-fight. Now Corbett aimed to be *world* champ. To win the title, he had to beat English champion Charley Mitchell.

But where to hold the fight? New York City was the obvious place. But legal problems came up. Corbett and Mitchell looked for a new city.

An athletic club in Jacksonville, Florida, finally offered to host the world championship fight. A special arena would be built for the occasion. And, for the first time, the boxers would follow the Marquis of Queensberry Rules.

These rules represented an effort by the boxing world to clean up its image. In the 1890s, boxing had a bad reputation as a brutal sport. Men would pound each other for as many as 75 rounds—or more. The Queensberry Rules made boxing more civilized. For one thing, the boxers were required to wear gloves.

But some people weren't convinced. They still thought that boxing was a disreputable sport. One of these critics was the governor of Florida, Henry Mitchell. He felt the fight would attract criminals. "They'd come to watch two fighters hammer each other until one is pounded into insensibility," he said.

Governor Mitchell vowed that the fight would never take place in his state. He ordered Sheriff Napoleon Bonapart Broward to see that it didn't.

Governor Mitchell also tried to stop the fighters from traveling by train to Jacksonville. He asked the railroads to stop running for 48 hours. But the railroads refused to comply. So Mitchell threatened to call up the state militia.

There were rumors that the fight would be moved. Some said it would be held in Waycross, Georgia.

The governor of Georgia, W.J. Norton, was also determined to keep the boxers and their low-life fans away. He sent 300 extra rifles to the state militia in Waycross.

As it turned out, W.J. Norton didn't have anything to worry about. All the trouble stayed in Florida.

Governor Mitchell was still against the match. Along with two companies of armed militiaman, he marched into downtown Jacksonville. But Jacksonville had a lot of boxing fans. Reports say that the governor and the militiamen were greeted with boos and hisses. Rocks and sandbags were thrown at them.

The athletic club struck back against the governor. It went to court—and won. The judge further ruled that Sheriff Napoleon Bonapart Broward could not prevent the fight.

Governor Mitchell was finally forced to back down.

On January 25, 1894, the fight took place. Tickets were priced at $25 and $10—a lot of money in those days. But the place was packed with 2,500 people. Among them were 300 sportswriters from around the world. Sheriff Broward refused to join the crowd. Instead, he waited outside, expecting trouble.

It wasn't an exciting fight. Corbett knocked out Mitchell in the third round. He won not only the world heavyweight championship, but a prize of $20,000.

But as Corbett and Mitchell left the

arena, Sheriff Broward arrested them on charges of assault and battery!

The charges were later dismissed, and the Englishman, Mitchell, disappeared from the boxing scene. Three years later, Corbett lost his title—but he wasn't washed up. Like many other athletes of the 1890s, he immediately went on to another career: show business.

And as for Sheriff Napoleon Bonapart Broward, he went on to be elected the next governor of Florida.

BASKETBALL

One of the oddest basketball games ever was played in 1982. Would you believe that a team of five players was beaten by a team of one?

That one player was Mike Lockhart, a six-foot-one-inch guard. Mike's team, the Knights, were probably feeling pretty good at the end of the first half. They were leading their rivals, the Sea Lions, by 15 points.

But the Knights ran into trouble early in the second half. One after another, they fouled out. And because of heavy illness and injuries, there were only three men on the bench! Midway through the second half, just four Knights were left to play. Yet, they held on to their lead.

As the nervous Knights' fans watched in horror, three more men fouled out! That left one player—Mike Lockhart. And the clock still showed 2 minutes and 10 seconds to go in the game.

Mike's team was leading: 70–57. According to the rules, a one-man team can continue the game—as long as that player's team is in the lead.

Mike was alone on the floor. "I was really scared," he said. "I could dribble the ball—but there was no one to pass to. And I had four fouls myself. If I made one more, the game would be over!" The worst part was inbounding the ball. After checking the rule book, the referee declared that the inbound ball must touch a player on the other team before Mike could go after it.

Mike inbounded the ball by bouncing it off a Sea Lion's leg. Then, with the clock ticking, he dribbled the ball. He was desperate to use up as much time as possible. Finally, he shot—and missed— but he grabbed his own rebound.

The Sea Lions couldn't believe that a single man was holding them off. Again and again, they tried to get the ball away from Mike. Three players made fouls. Mike got six freethrows—and put five of them through the hoop!

When the Sea Lions finally managed to get the ball, their game was falling apart. One man missed an easy shot. Another player was called for traveling. And two wild Sea Lions passes sent the ball out of bounds. They managed to score only ten points.

The final score was Knights: 75, Sea Lions: 67. Believe it or not, Mike Lockhart had won a five-on-one game!

HORSE RACING

A steeplechase race is tough and dangerous. Along the course, horses and jockeys must clear fences, hedges, and ditches. It's not unusual for horses to fall. In one memorable race, a horse did happen to fall—and a moment later a truly unbelievable thing happened.

This amazing race took place in 1953, at England's famous Southwell racetrack. A horse named Royal Student was the favorite to win.

At the fifth fence, Royal Student was in the lead. Knother, a horse ridden by Mick Morrissey, was right behind him. Then suddenly, Royal Student crashed, and his jockey was thrown to the ground. Unable to stop, Knother slammed into Royal Student—and Mick Morrissey was thrown high into the air.

Just as Royal Student was struggling to his feet, Mick plopped down on Royal Student's saddle! It didn't matter that Royal Student finished the race last. No

one who was at the track that day will ever forget that legendary event. Jockey Mick Morrissey started the race on one horse and finished on another!

THE OLYMPICS

There are many extraordinary stories about Olympic athletes. Felix Carvajal's story is definitely one of the strangest.

A postal worker in Havana, Cuba, Felix was excited to hear that the 1904 Olympics would be held in the United States. He knew he was a good, strong runner. Why not run in the Olympic marathon? Felix had never entered a competitive race in his life. But that didn't stop him. His dream was to win a gold medal for Cuba!

In order to train for the race, Felix quit his job at the post office. But he had no money to travel to the Olympic venue in St. Louis, Missouri. He made a plan.

To attract attention, he ran around a public square in Havana. When a big crowd gathered to watch, Felix told them about his dream and asked for donations. After running laps around the square for several days, he finally had enough money for the trip.

On the first leg of his journey, a ship took him to New Orleans. There, he lost all his money in a crooked dice game! But Felix was still determined to make it to the Olympics. He walked and hitchhiked 700 miles to St. Louis! Along the way, he told his story to sympathetic strangers who bought him food.

Felix arrived just a few days before the marathon race. The long trip had left him ragged, exhausted, and half-starved. Luckily, the United States weight-lifting team took pity on him. They fed him and gave him a place to sleep.

The day of the marathon, Felix joined the other runners. They all stared at him. He was wearing heavy walking shoes, a long-sleeved shirt and long pants! The race was delayed while another athlete cut off Felix's pants at the knee.

Then the starter's gun fired and the 31 runners took off. The temperature was over 90 degrees, and the air was heavy and sticky. But these conditions didn't bother Felix. He laughed and joked about it. Along the way he practiced speaking English with friendly bystanders. At one point, he spotted two Olympic officials in a car. They were about to bite into some peaches. Reaching through the car window, Felix swiped the peaches out of their hands! Farther along the course he paused at an orchard and picked some apples. Unfortunately, the green apples gave him stomach cramps, which slowed him down a bit.

Only 14 runners finished the race. Against all odds, Felix Carvajal came in fourth. If he hadn't stopped for a couple of snacks, he might have actually won the Olympic Marathon!

TWO TERRIBLE SHIPWRECKS

A "REAL LIFE" NOVEL

In 1898, Morgan Robertson published a poorly written novel called *Futility*. Very few people read it. The story was a thinly veiled warning about luxury oceanliners. Robertson felt that ship companies cared more for money than their passengers' lives.

The ship in Robertson's story was enormous—by far the largest ever built. Its passengers, about 3,000 of them, were rich and famous. Its maiden voyage took place on a calm April night. Halfway across the Atlantic Ocean, it struck an iceberg—and sank. Many, many lives were lost in the icy water.

As an innovative safety feature, Robertson's fictional ship had 19 watertight compartments. Water in one compartment could not travel to the next.

The big ship also had three propellers.

Fourteen years after Robertson's novel was published, a real oceanliner was built. It was the largest ever constructed. In many ways, it was exactly like the ship in the novel.

Both were about 800 feet long and weighed between 60 and 70 tons. The real ship was the first to actually have three propellers. Both ships were supplied with only enough lifeboats for a small number of passengers. Why? Like the ship in the novel, the real ship was thought to be "unsinkable."

The real ship set off from England on April 10, 1912. Among her passengers were some of the richest and most famous people in the world. Halfway across the Atlantic Ocean, on a calm night, the ship struck an iceberg—and sank. Some 1,513 lives were lost in the icy waters of the Atlantic.

The real ship was the *Titanic*. The ship in Robertson's novel was called the *Titan*.

THE MIRACLE GIRL

It was July 25, 1956. The Italian luxury liner, *Andrea Doria,* was headed from Italy to New York. There were several famous people on board that day, including well-known actors. One of her passengers was 14-year-old Linda Morgan. She was not famous—yet. Not long after dinner, Linda went to her cabin and fell asleep.

While Linda slept, the *Andrea Doria* sailed into disaster.

People said that the *Andrea Doria* was the safest ship ever. Its safety features included watertight compartments and fireproof walls that divided the ship into three safety zones. Furthermore, the 16 lifeboats could hold all the ship's passengers—and more.

The *Andrea Doria* was also famous for its beauty and luxury. It had bars, libraries, gyms, and areas set aside for movies and dancing. The ship was richly decorated with murals, tapestries, and rare woods. It also had the latest

technology, including air conditioning.

About 11:00 that night, people were dancing in the lounge when the crew noticed another ship approaching. According to the radar screen, it was several miles away. The other ship, a Swedish liner called the *Stockholm*, had also noticed the *Andrea Doria*. One of the officers on the *Stockholm* looked through his binoculars. Oh, no! The *Andrea Doria* was right in front of them! He yelled for the ship to turn sharply.

The captain of the *Andrea Doria* made a quick turn, too. Then the unthinkable happened. The bow of the *Stockholm* rammed right into the *Andrea Doria*!

Built for breaking up icebergs, the bow of the *Stockholm* was strong. It sliced through the side of the *Andrea Doria* as if it were made of butter. It tore away more than 300 tons of steel, and ripped a 75-foot gash. As water poured in, the *Andrea Doria* rolled on its side. The lights flickered, then went out. Frightened passengers in evening clothes and pajamas ran through dark passageways.

Both ships sent distress signals, and other ships raced to help. The *Stockholm*'s crew helped rescue many of the *Andrea Doria*'s passengers. Thanks to so many rescuers, 1,660 passengers and crew of the *Andrea Doria* survived. At the moment of impact, however, 51 people had died.

After the rescue, the crew of the *Stockholm* checked over their ship for damage. Bernabé Garcia was checking the ship's bow. It was covered with broken-off pieces of the *Andrea Doria*. Then suddenly, he heard cries for help. He made his way through the wreckage and saw a smashed bed on top of a mattress. On the bed was Linda Morgan!

When Garcia reached her, she asked, "Where am I? What ship is this?"

The crew of the *Stockholm* checked its passenger list. Linda Morgan's name wasn't there. It took a while before anyone knew just how she'd ended up on the *Stockholm*'s bow. But this is what happened: The bow of the *Stockholm* rammed into the *Andrea Doria* just below Linda's bed! Then the *Stockholm* had pulled back from the *Andrea Doria*, taking Linda and her bed with it. Hours later, and miles away from the *Andrea Doria*, she woke up.

Linda had some injuries, but she was alive. The man who found her, Bernabé Garcia, visited her in the hospital. He touched her cheek and smiled. "It is a miracle," he whispered. The newspapers, too, called her the "miracle girl."

KING TUT'S CURSE

Pharaoh Tutankhamen, the boy king, became the ruler of ancient Egypt at age 9. He was only 18 or 19 years old when he died. The cause of his death is still a mystery.

The rumors began in 1922 when Tut's tomb was discovered. Supposedly, hieroglyphic writing warned that anyone who disturbed Tut's tomb would face terrible punishment.

Two Englishmen had found the tomb: Howard Carter, an archeologist, and Lord Carnarvon, who'd paid for the expeditions.

Carter had been searching Egypt's Valley of Kings for more than ten years. Then, in November 1922, he, Carnarvon, and their workers were digging near the tomb of King Ramses VI. They pulled debris away from the entrance of the tomb and found a door! Excited, Carter and Carnarvon stepped through the entrance. Until now, every tomb they'd found had been looted by robbers. This one seemed untouched.

They lit a match—and saw the gleam of gold. They saw fabulous necklaces, earrings, bracelets, and rings.

The tomb contained four chambers. Inside were chariots, thrones, swords, shields—even fans made of ostrich feathers. There were figures of animals, models of ships, toys and games. There were also practical items such as linens and clothes. Since Egyptians believed in life after death, called the *afterlife*, their belongings were buried with them.

Carter and Carnarvon realized they'd finally found King Tut's tomb! But many believed the discovery was accompanied by bad omens. At the moment Carter entered the tomb, his canary was eaten. A cobra, an Egyptian symbol of royalty, had slithered into his home and devoured the bird.

In London, Carnarvon's dog died.

Then Carnarvon himself died of an infected mosquito bite. According to some stories, when Tut's mummy was unwrapped, it had a wound on its left cheek. Carnarvon was bitten by the mosquito in exactly the same spot.

From then on, every time a member of the expedition died, people said it was proof of the mummy's curse.

Or was it? Carnarvon's death was partly his fault. His razor nicked the mosquito bite when he shaved. The bite became infected, but Carnarvon ignored it. He caught pneumonia, and died. Yet, somehow, this doesn't seem like the "terrible punishment" the hieroglyphics warned of.

And nothing awful happened to Carter. He lived until the age of 66.

Yet the canary really did die. In 1977, Egypt's head of antiquities was hit and killed by a car. This was after he agreed to let 70 objects from King Tut's tomb travel to Great Britain. So perhaps it *is* risky to disturb the tomb of a king!

THE INCREDIBLE CATCH

The night of July 27, 1981, Tom Deal felt terrible. He'd played softball with a local Chicago team that afternoon. All his team had needed to win was for the other team to make one more out.

Then a batter on the other team hit a fly ball—straight to Deal. It should have been an easy catch. But the ball bounced off Deal's glove.

The other team went on to score five runs. They won the game—all because Deal had flubbed the catch.

That night he went to sleep brooding about the missed catch.

The next morning, he woke to the sound of a baby crying. Deal and his wife, Lorri, looked out their bedroom window.

Just across the way was another apartment building. On the third floor, ten-month-old Jennifer Deul was crying.

Unfortunately, her babysitter was asleep.

As Deal and Lorri watched, little Jennifer worked open the screen door. Then she crept out toward the edge of the balcony. What if she tried to crawl under the railing?

Deal threw on a bathrobe. He raced to the other apartment building and pushed the buzzer on the door of the third-floor apartment. There was no answer.

Deal could still hear Jennifer crying, so he ran out to the corner and looked up. Both of Jennifer's feet were under the railing! When Jennifer fell, head-over-heels toward the ground, Tom Deal was waiting below.

As the baby bounced off the second floor railing bar, Deal dove forward and caught her under one armpit.

Tom Deal had made the most important catch of his life!

MONSTERS

BIGFOOT

Americans call it *Bigfoot*, Canadians call it *Sasquatch*, and the Sherpas of Nepal call it *Yeti*. All agree it's huge and hairy, part animal and part human. Hundreds of people swear they've seen these creatures. But many other people don't believe they exist at all.

Native Americans tell stories of human-like creatures roaming the land before white people came to North America. Early settlers in northern California have seen them. There have also been reports of Bigfoot sightings in Ohio and Florida.

In China, there are reports of a hairy "wild man." In Russia, people claim to have seen the "Snow Person."

Here's a typical story of a sighting. This one happened on March 18, 1987, in

British Columbia, Canada. A seven-man oil crew was working in the wilderness when four of the crew saw a monster. They claimed it stood about 7 feet tall and weighed about 400 pounds. "The thing looked more like a man than an animal," said one of the workers, Myles Jack.

The monster crouched down and watched the men. Then it circled the worksite. Jack said, "It looked like we were in his territory and he was checking us out. He seemed really curious."

Another worker, Bryan Mestdagh, said, "I've seen a documentary on the Sasquatch. I'd have to say that what we saw was absolutely identical."

Another famous sighting was in 1958. It took place near the town of Willow Creek, in northern California. Jerry Crew, a bulldozer operator, was working there with a road-building crew.

On the morning of August 27, Crew noticed footprints in the dirt near his bulldozer. Figuring they were bear tracks, he climbed onto the bulldozer and looked down. Now he could see that the tracks approached the bulldozer, made a circle around it and went off into the forest. The prints were larger than anything he'd ever seen.

Crew jumped down from the bulldozer. He compared one of his own feet to one of the prints—and broke out in goose bumps. The prints were *enormous*.

Crew showed the prints to his foreman, Wilbur Wallace. The foreman had a story of his own. He said that he'd also seen the huge prints.

Crew made a plaster-of-Paris cast of one of the prints and took it into town. Soon dozens of news stories were written about Crew's discovery.

In 2002, when Wilbur Wallace died, his family revealed a secret. Wilbur had made an enormous foot out of wood. He'd taken it to the worksite and laid down the tracks Crew had found. The whole Bigfoot sighting in Willow Creek was a fake!

But are all the sightings fakes? Many argue that the big tracks are made by bears. They say the bears have simply overstepped their front paw mark. And others insist that sightings prove nothing. Eyewitness accounts are often unreliable, they point out. This has been proven again and again in law courts.

No fossils of Bigfoot have been found. But fossils do not form in wet, acidic soil. The Pacific Northwest, where Bigfoot is said to roam, has wet, acidic soil.

Some well-respected scientists believe Bigfoot could be real. Jane Goodall, famous for studying chimpanzees in Africa, is certain that Bigfoot exists.

Another scientist is Jeff Meldrum, from Idaho State University. He says every Bigfoot sighting can't be dismissed as a fake. He also thinks that some of the footprints seem to be real. A few samples of Bigfoot's hair have been found. These hair samples can't be matched to any known animal.

In 2000, a huge plaster cast of a Bigfoot creature was made from a muddy impression discovered near a pond. Several scientists were impressed by the cast. Jeff Meldrum said that if the cast is a fake, it is a masterpiece. Daris Swindler, a professor from the University of Washington, didn't believe in Bigfoot's existence. But when he saw the plaster cast, he, too, was impressed. He said it would be difficult to fake.

So perhaps Bigfoot *does* exist. Until bones or a body are found, however, we cannot know for sure.

THE LOCH NESS MONSTER

Loch Ness is a lake in northern Scotland. It is large enough, and deep enough, to hide something big. But is there really a "monster" lurking in the lake? Many people think so.

As far back as A.D. 565, there were reports of a strange creature in Loch Ness. Throughout the 1900s there were several sightings of the huge creature.

When the road near the lake was upgraded in 1933, sightings grew more and more frequent. In May 1933, Mr. and Mrs. Mackay reported seeing some strange disturbances in the water. Two months later, tourists from London, the Spicers, saw something in the bushes by the road. Mr. Spicer said, "The body shot across the road in jerks. It was about 5 feet in height. I estimate the length to be 25–30 feet."

In December 1933, a newspaper sponsored a hunt for the monster, which was nicknamed "Nessie." A big-game hunter discovered a giant footprint near the lake. But the print turned out to be a fake. Someone had made the impression with a dried hippopotamus foot!

In 1934, Dr. Robert Wilson took a famous photograph of Nessie. The image was fuzzy, but there was no mistaking the monster. The picture showed a huge aquatic reptile with a long curved neck. The creature looked like a plesiosaurus.

For many years, people believed this must be Nessie. Then, in 1994, the photograph was analyzed with high-tech equipment. It turned out to be a toy boat with a plastic model in it!

Many sightings, in fact, have turned out to be fakes. But others have encouraged Nessie's "believers."

In 1960, an aircraft engineer named Tim Dinsdale made a short film. It shows a dark shape moving through the waters of Loch Ness. Experts from Britain's Royal Air Force analyzed Dinsdale's film. They said the dark shape was probably a living creature.

Several scientists have explored the lake. They searched for Nessie using sonar. (Sonar uses sound to detect underwater objects.) Sonar *did* detect large moving objects in the lake. But the reading couldn't tell if it was one large body or a very big school of fish.

People continue to spot the monster. Ian Cameron, for example, was on the lake fishing with a friend of his one day.

He saw something break the surface of the water. He kept watching as it disappeared, then broke the surface again. "It was a whale-like object," he said.

Several people who had gathered by the lake were also watching. "I can't compare it to anything I ever saw before," Cameron reported. "We all had an emotional attraction to it—there was no fear at all."

Cameron has a dim view of scientists. He says if they can't "pigeon-hole" something, they dismiss it. But along with many, many others, Cameron has an answer for them. "I *saw* it," he insists. So the mystery of the Loch Ness monster is still unsolved.

DEADLY ADDRESSES

50 BERKELEY SQUARE

Number 50 Berkeley Square is a house in a fashionable part of London. It was built in the late 18th century. For a long time, people thought it was the most dangerous haunted house in England.

The building acquired its dreadful reputation in the 1830s. That's when a maid went insane in her bedroom. The story goes that her madness was caused by fright. One magazine said she was "found standing in the middle of her room." She was as "rigid as a corpse, with hideously glaring eyes, unable to speak." Supposedly, she died the next day in an insane asylum.

Never again did the family go in the maid's room. One day, though, a visitor challenged the family. He vowed to sleep in the "haunted" room. But that night, the family heard him screaming. They rushed into the room and found him dead.

The coroner's report said the visitor had been "frightened to death."

In 1859, Mr. Myers rented the place. The story goes that Myers was about to be married. He planned to bring his bride to 50 Berkeley Square.

Just before the wedding, though, his fiancée broke off the engagement. And Myers went insane.

He let the building fall into disrepair and never went outside. He stayed in one small room and wouldn't answer the door—except for a servant bringing him food or water.

People said Myers walked the house at night, holding a candle. He wept and called out the name of his lost fiancée.

For a long time, no one lived in the house. Then, in 1887, two sailors from the frigate *HMS Penelope* were in town. They were looking for a place to stay for the night. Noticing that 50 Berkeley Square

appeared to be empty, they let themselves in and went to sleep.

In the middle of the night, the sailors heard footsteps outside their room. Then a "thing" entered the room and attacked them. The "thing" was later described as a white-faced man with a gaping mouth. One of the sailors tried to fight the intruder off with a curtain rod.

The other man raced outside. He found a police officer and dragged him back to the house. Just outside, they found the other sailor—dead. It looked as if he had fallen out the bedroom window. Or had he been pushed? A look of horror was frozen on his face.

In the 1870s and 1880s the house was far from quiet. Neighbors reported hearing loud noises, cries, and moans. They also heard bells ringing and something like stones and books being thrown around.

In the early 1900s, the house was supposedly exorcised. Since then it's been fairly quiet. In 1938, the building became the Maggs Brothers bookstore. The owner, John Maggs, hasn't had any experience with ghosts. But his staff, and even Mrs. Maggs, make no such claim. They say that every now and then something too weird to be explained happens in the store.

THE TOWER OF LONDON

The Tower of London has been used as a prison, an arsenal, a zoo, a treasury, and a mint! It has also been a place to die. Hundreds—perhaps even thousands—of people have been executed there. Some say the spirits of these dead people are still roaming the tower.

The Tower was built about 900 years ago. Over the years, many buildings have been added. These days the tower is more like a castle or fortress.

Horse thieves and smugglers were sometimes executed at the tower. And so were royalty.

Usually, ordinary people died in public. They were executed in front of a noisy crowd. Royalty, though, were executed in private. Often they had committed no crime. In most cases, an enemy in the royal family just wanted to get rid of them!

This was the case for two young princes. Richard, Duke of York, was ten years old. His brother, twelve-year-old Edward V, was heir to the throne. In 1483, the boys were imprisoned in the tower. They were murdered in secret. Most people believe that their uncle was behind the crime. Why? With both boys gone, the uncle became King Richard III.

Many people say they've seen the ghosts of the two young boys. They usually appear standing together, hand in hand. Reports say they have sad, lost looks on their faces.

Anne Boleyn was another famous prisoner of the tower. Henry VIII had divorced his first wife to marry Anne. The divorce, however, hurt the king's reputation. But three years after marrying Anne, he grew tired of her. Not wanting to go through another divorce, he imprisoned Anne in the tower. Then she was executed—while Henry went on to marry four more wives!

The ghost of Anne Boleyn has been seen many, many times. One sighting happened in 1864. The Captain of the Guard was making his rounds when he spotted one of his men on the ground, unconscious. Underneath him lay his rifle, with its bayonet in place.

When the man woke up, he said he'd seen a figure in white. She'd come out of the room where Anne Boleyn had spent her last night.

The ghostly figure had glided up to him. Frightened, he ordered it to stop— but it kept on coming. In a panic, he stabbed at the figure with his bayonet— but the weapon went straight through the spirit's body! The guard fainted.

The captain didn't believe the guard's story. He claimed the guard had been sleeping while on duty, so he court-martialed him. But several other guards came forward during the trial. They, too, said they'd seen the ghostly woman.

The guard was set free.

Catherine Howard was Henry VIII's fifth wife. Like Anne Boleyn, she was executed in the tower. But just before her death, she escaped from her cell. She ran down a corridor, frantically looking for a way out. But there was no way out and no one to help her. She was caught, returned to her cell, and executed. People say that her ghost is always seen running in a panic down that corridor.

Lady Jane Gray was only 16 when she became queen in 1553. She ruled for nine short days before her cousin, Mary Tudor, overthrew her. Mary ordered Gray and her husband to be executed.

Lady Jane's ghost has been seen many times—most often on the anniversary of her death. Her husband's weeping figure has also been seen standing beside her.

Most of the Tower of London ghosts are spirits of those who died there. But more than one sighting is related to the Crown Jewels. Owned by the royal family, they include crowns, scepters, and other items that were once worn by monarchs and their children. One crown, called the Imperial State Crown, is set with 2,868 diamonds, 17 sapphires, 11 emeralds, 5 rubies, and 273 pearls.

The Crown Jewels are kept in the Jewel Tower and guarded around the clock. It is said that in the year 1800, about midnight, a guard in the Jewel Tower sensed something behind him. He turned and saw an enormous black bear.

The bear reared up on its hind legs, snarling. What happened next was similar to the sighting of Anne Boleyn's ghost. The guard struck at the bear with his bayonet. Then, when the bayonet passed through the ghostly body, the terrified guard fainted dead away.

The guard was taken to the hospital. Unfortunately, he never recovered from the shock. He died a few days later.

Today, the tower is one of Britain's most popular tourist attractions. People come to admire the Crown Jewels. And they walk the steps that Anne Boleyn, Catherine Howard, and many others walked—to their doom. No doubt some visitors hope to see one of these restless spirits as they take the tour!

CROP CIRCLES

In the movie *Signs*, Mel Gibson's character wakes one morning to an amazing sight. Overnight, an enormous design has appeared on his cornfield!

What he sees is a crop circle—a design made when wheat or corn is swept down to form a pattern.

More than 5,000 of these patterns have been seen in more than 40 countries. Most of them, though, appear in England. Some designs are astonishing. There are crops circles in the shape of mazes, spinning wheels, and maps of the planets. Some designs are simple, and some are as complex as a snowflake.

Many believe that crop circles are made by aliens. But many more believe they're made by jolts of energy from the earth. Others conclude that crop circles are simply an unsolved mystery.

Do you think crop circles are a hoax—the work of pranksters? In 1991, two British men confessed that they'd made crop circles all over England. Wooden boards pulled by ropes were used to make the patterns.

Matthew Williams was arrested for trespassing on a farmer's field in 2001. He says making crop circles isn't hard. "All you need is a pencil, a compass, and a ruler to design it on paper," he says.

Peter Sorensen from California said that he and his friends have made about a dozen crop circles. They designed them on computers.

Some people, however, insist that crop circles, especially the complicated ones, *can't* be made in one night.

William Gazecki, a documentary filmmaker, said, "How many man-hours would it take to make a perfect crop circle, with no mistakes? The summer nights in England are only four to five hours long. It takes me five hours just to *draw* one of these things. How could they do all that work with ropes and planks in the dark?"

One design, discovered in July 1996, was called the "Triple Julia Set." Nearly 1,000 feet long, it was made up of 700 perfect circles. Another design, called the "Galaxy Spiral Arm," was spread over 11 acres of wheat. It was made up of 409 circles. Could such enormous, perfectly drawn designs be made overnight?

One crop circle *was* made on the evening of July 7, 1996. The pilot of a small plane passed over a field. Half an hour later, when he flew back the same way, a huge, complicated design had appeared on the field. It was 900 feet long and 500 feet wide!

Many insist that at least some crop circles are not made by humans. They wonder why the stalks of grain are bent, but never broken. Why are crackling sounds heard near crop circles? And why have so many people seen strange "balls

of light" just before the patterns appear?

Ron Russell has seen one such "ball of light." "It was like a planet," he said, "but too bright to be a planet. It went straight above us before it disappeared."

Jim Lyons, an engineer, says the plants in crop circles show changes in their nitrogen levels. After testing flattened crops, he says the electrical fields around them often seem to be disturbed.

Yet some think such research is nonsense.

Michael Glickman gives lectures on crop circles. He believes most crop circles are not fakes. "But who cares how they do it?" he says. "If the circles are made by people, I'd love to meet them. They must have very beautiful minds."

MIND OVER MATTER

Uri Geller says he uses his mind to bend metal. When he strokes a metal fork, it bends. Even after he takes his hand away, the metal keeps moving.

Geller says he has the power of *psychokinesis*. That means he can move objects with his thoughts.

In the 1970s, Uri Geller was famous. He often appeared on TV, bending metal and stopping clocks. He described drawings that were hidden in envelopes. A novel, a board game, and a record were based on him. He appeared on the covers of 400 magazines, and 20 books were written about him.

Geller, an Israeli, grew up in a poor part of Tel Aviv. His mother was a seamstress. His father was in the military. Unfortunately, when Geller was ten, his parents divorced.

In an interview, Geller remembered his parents' divorce as a painful time. It was then that he created a fantasy world where he had total control. He dreamed of being rich and famous.

As an adult, Geller worked in a women's clothing factory. There, he met a photographer. Eager to show off his metal-bending talent, Geller bent a ring for him. Impressed, the photographer invited Geller to a party.

As Geller tells it, "I was quite a hit. After that the parties got better and better. First they were for businessmen and army officers. Then judges and lawyers came to see me."

In 1969, he met the prime minister of Israel, Golda Meir. Later, when Meir was on a radio show, someone asked her about the future of Israel. "Don't ask me," she said. "Ask Geller." After this remark by Golda Meir, Geller's fame skyrocketed. Suddenly, everyone wanted to interview him, or to demonstrate his feats on TV.

Geller said he was especially loved by Israelis after the Six-Day War in 1967. "The country was in a depressed state," he said. "In me they found a happy outlet." Grieving mothers would beg him to get in touch with their dead sons.

Geller moved to England as his fame was spreading around the globe. Spoon bending had made him a celebrity in every country in the world. He had a 1976 Cadillac with more than 5,000 bent spoons attached to it. Many of the spoons were given to him by celebrities. A few of these famous people were Winston Churchill, John Kennedy, Elvis Presley, the Duchess of Windsor, and the famous Beatle, John Lennon.

As Geller's fame grew, some people accused him of being a fraud. James Randi, an American magician, doesn't believe in Geller's powers at all. He insists that Geller is a magician, not a psychic. Geller's tricks are not that hard to do, he claims.

At the height of his fame, Geller was planning to be in a Hollywood movie. Then a producer, Robert Stigwood, told him that he needed to lose some weight. As the Israeli told it later, Stigwood's words triggered a terrible reaction. Geller became bulimic. Finally, his doctor warned him that if he didn't eat normally, he would die.

After quitting show business, Geller wrote books about positive thinking. He also used his powers to search for gold, oil, and minerals. In recent years, he's occasionally appeared on TV. According to Geller, a number of world leaders ask him for advice.

These days he lives very comfortably in a mansion in England. "When I was a boy," he said, "I had no bed, so I had to sleep in a cupboard. Now I've got 12 paintings by Dali and six servants. Important men often ring me up to ask about world peace. How many people can say that?"

HE SAW THE FUTURE

In 1503, Nostradamus was born in France. His birth name was Michel de Nostredame.

At school, Nostradamus studied to be a doctor. In those days, astrology was a required subject for medical students. Nostradamus studied the subject more thoroughly than anyone.

When Nostradamus became a doctor, he helped victims of the bubonic plague. This disease, also called the Black Death, killed millions of people in Europe and Asia. At that time, doctors had only useless remedies to offer. One of these was bleeding their patients to get rid of "bad blood."

Nostradamus's cure actually *helped* many plague victims. He told them to drink clean water and get plenty of fresh air. He also gave them his special pills.

71

These contained sawdust from cypress trees, cloves, aloe, and powdered rose petals. (Rose petals are full of vitamin C.)

His success with plague victims seemed to be astonishing. But when his wife and children died from the plague, people turned against him. Soon he was ordered to stand trial. His crime? He had made a humorous remark about demons several years earlier.

Nostradamus did not want to stand trial. So he packed up his belongings and disappeared. Ten years later, he returned. At last his reputation had been restored—but not as a doctor. This time, Nostradamus had become famous for his predictions.

One of his predictions concerned the King of France, Henry II. He predicted Henry's death in a verse:

The young lion shall overcome the old
In warlike fields in a single duel;
In a cage of gold he will pierce his eyes,
Two wounds one, then die, a cruel death.

Four years later, in 1559, it happened. Henry II died in a jousting tournament (*in warlike fields in a single duel*). His opponent was a younger man (*the young lion overcoming the old*).

The younger man's spear splintered and wounded Henry in two places (*two wounds*). Part of the spear hit the king's throat, and the other part went though his golden helmet (*the cage of gold*) and pierced his eye (*he will pierce his eyes*). Henry died that night.

That prediction added new luster to Nostradamus's reputation.

Many people wondered if he was a witch who'd planned to kill the king. But other powerful people were on his side. After inviting Nostradamus to Paris, Queen Catherine made him her personal astrologer. King Charles IX chose him as his doctor. Royalty from all over Europe listened to his predictions.

No one knows how Nostradamus made his predictions. It is known that he

learned where the stars and planets were on certain dates. Then, perhaps, he figured out how likely events in the past—such as wars, earthquakes, and plagues—were to take place once again.

The predictions of Nostradamus were collected in a book called *Centuries*. The book was supposed to foretell the future of the world. It isn't easy to read, because Nostradamus used several languages in his writing. It's also difficult to figure out what ideas he was trying to convey. Hundreds of books have been written to interpret his writings.

Many of his predictions turned out to be correct. He predicted Louis Pasteur's discoveries and the date of the great London fire (1666). He predicted many events of the French Revolution.

According to many interpreters, Nostradamus predicted Hitler's rise to power and World War II. During the war, the Nazis used their interpretations of *Centuries* as propaganda. They also claimed he'd predicted a Nazi victory. Nazi planes dropped copies of these predictions over Belgium and France.

The British fought back with their own propaganda. Their interpretation of *Centuries* predicted a victory for the British and the other Allies. They, too, dropped leaflets over Belgium and France.

Nostradamus predicted his own death, at age 63. In 1566, he wrote: *"He will be found dead near the bed and the bench."*

A few months later, his family found his body. He was lying across a bench he used to help him get out of bed.

The predictions of Nostradamus are still read today. *Centuries*, in fact, is one of the few books that have remained in print for hundreds of years!